LET'S SKIP
THE BULL

LESSONS FROM
DAD AFTER
YOUR MOM DIED

Daryl Calfee

First Print Edition, 2025

Publishing Services: Jodi Cowles, Brandon Janous, and Rachael Mitchell (Blue Hat Publishing)
Cover Design: Daryl Calfee
Interior Layout: Daryl Calfee and Paige Elliott (Blue Hat Publishing)

ISBN: 978-1-962674-46-1

This book is dedicated to the three little people
I believe could make a big impact in our world:
my children—Ella, Easton, and Emmanuel. You carry
your mother's spirit, humor, and beauty.

CONTENTS

FAITH + DEATH

WORK + MONEY

ACKNOWLEDGMENTS

HELLO
I LOVE YOU.
-DAD

To my kids: I know you won't remember most of the conversations we have on a daily basis. I know this because I don't remember the important conversations I had as a kid either. No one does, or at least very few. As a kid, you mostly remember experiences and places. You will remember our home(s), a few key vacation trips, and moments at school or camps. You will remember your first love and your first fight, and you will remember standing in front of your mom as she died. It will be burned into your brain and your heart. But the conversations? The daily conversations with me, your dad, you will not remember, so I am writing them here for you to reflect on one day when you're a mom yourself, a sister who needs comfort, a boy trying to become a man. One day you will need these conversations, so I am preserving them here for you.

As your Dad, I want you to know that I have not been perfect, but I have made my own way. I've failed. I've won. I've learned by not knowing and figuring it out. You will do the same, but please take the faster path that I have helped to mark ahead of you. Realize that your own life is very short and all that will remain is what you imprint on the hearts and minds of those you touch. Make it count. Your mom did that. In her too-short time here, she made her mark on those around us, even across the world. In her last months alive, she wanted to make you videos and write her thoughts for you to carry, but unfortunately her body became so weak that she just could not gather the energy to do it all. In fact, you will probably remember her last weekend with you. . . .

It's Saturday, August 26, 2023.

Johanna is at Ella's + Pop Pop's birthday, celebrating.
The next day she can't get off the sofa.
Monday morning her body is shutting down, she cannot dress herself. I wheel her into the oncology center for the last time.

This may even be the last book you read. That awareness will either freeze you with fear or energize you to take immediate action; my hope for you is the latter.

Tuesday she is mostly unresponsive—family/friends come to sit with her while hospice care arrives.

Wednesday morning—6 a.m.—she has passed away peacefully, and my children say goodbye to their mother.

The problem is, you will think you have time.

You don't.

Stop waiting. Worrying. Hoping the right time or thing will come along. Truth is, for someone, this is their last weekend. This may even be the last book you read. That awareness will either freeze you with fear or energize you to take immediate action; my hope for you is the latter.

In light of her death, which stole her hopes and dreams of leaving a written legacy for you, I am picking up the torch to finish what I know she wanted for you: a basic guide to help you when you find yourself feeling lost. This map will be more like a keepsake box of words and experiences from my own life—a stockpile of handed-down wisdom from those mentors who poured into me (and your mother) over the years.

And as for you, the reader: *Many of us don't remember detailed conversations with our parents that we had as kids.* We have a few core memories locked away, perhaps a couple of key conversations, but for the most part, they are lost in the base layer of our childhood and teen years.

Do it. Try to recall more than a handful now. Anything come to mind? I bet you didn't get past six dialogues, and if you did, you are a rare bird.

So may you find these personal notations funny, reflective, and maybe even helpful for your own journey. Perhaps you will hear the heart of this one father, and it will be the spark you needed to stop talking and start doing. Or perhaps, as an adult, you will reframe the experiences and conversations of your childhood in a positive way.

I quit my job. For more than twenty years, I had been in the world of design and marketing, but with Johanna still battling cancer and three kids at home, I knew where I was needed most.

Trust me, no kid ever grows up wanting to be a marketing director. I was just a kid who loved to draw—on paper, on his walls, in the pews of Sunday night church. I literally had poster boards of logos for imaginary companies. It was when I sold my first piece of art in the 7th grade to Ms. Carrier (my art teacher— God bless her $20) that the worlds of commerce and creativity collided for me. My "work" had a value. My entrepreneurial spirit and creative nature came together with that first $20 sale of a triangular figure—it launched me. In the first twenty years of my career, I was a designer, photographer, art director, and marketing executive—all roles in which I was paid to produce creative content. Creative work and managing creatives are a large part of who I am—and creativity is a large part of my kids. I see it already. They are makers—art, pottery, stories, and video— it's bone-deep for them.

Being a creative in the workplace is often like being on an island in the middle of a bubble: There are boundaries and edges, but often you feel alone or in a very small tribe—yet somehow still in a bubble you can see. You sit outside but inside the organization. Sometimes you will find an agency or creative shop where you truly feel at home, but the pay sucks, so you launch out on your own or go back to a corporate marketing team. One scares you, the other can dull your edges.

No approach to creative work is right or wrong, but keep in mind that's what it is—work. Here are some lessons I've learned along the way that I wish I had known earlier in my creative career.

Leaders Write (and Read)—I Didn't Until I Was Almost Thirty

We were once asked in a men's group, "What do great leaders have in common?" The room was filled with smart answers about leadership, communication, and bravery. As the group talked through it, an obvious common habit emerged: Leaders write. Great leaders throughout history have written. Are there other similarities between admirable leaders? Sure, but a common thread is that they write. St. Paul, George Washington, Marie Curie, Rosa Parks, MLK—they all wrote. Their leadership continues because they wrote. In the same spirit, journal your thoughts, your perspective, your meeting agenda, and your notes. Write on a laptop, on paper, on your tablet—but write! Your mom was one of the best writers (and editors) I ever met. She was fast, sharp, and always witty. When she died, I expected to find a book—this book, the book she left behind for us to follow and learn what she was really thinking as she wrestled with life, faith, and death toward the end.

But she did not.

So she will be found in these words to you. In a way, through me, you will also hear from her. >

Reading was a $21.99 cheat code that gave me tools and language I never had before...

There is no other purchase of $15–25 that will change your life, I promise.

I am ashamed to say I only read about three books in my entire life before age thirty. I wouldn't even read IKEA instructions, I scanned those. That is, until I had to read in order to save myself and my marriage. I was asked to read a book on sexual abuse victims and their hearts. It changed mine. Your mom was a victim of sexual abuse, and it laid waste to her heart. It made it hard for her to find connection and trust. So in order to save our marriage, I had some learning to do. That book unlocked something for me. It was powerful. It was a $21.99 cheat code that gave me tools and language I never had before. From there, it has been a life of learning through reading. Read anything, read everything. Read for fun, read for vacation, read to learn something new, and even read to save someone you love.

There is no other purchase of $15–25 that will change your life, I promise.

Find good mentors and friendships where you can trust the other person's counsel. Listen. Apply. Retry.

Visit the Sea Often

Tears. Sweat. Seawater. Salt water is good for the soul and your creative spirit.

Set specific dates each year to visit the shore. Use the time to recharge and rethink creative problems. I promise you will find clarity.

Go for a walk, run, or sit on the worn wood steps and watch the waves. Their frequency will release something in your brain. The interesting thing about the sea is that it brings you something new every time.

We have done this for years with friends during New Year's. It has become my favorite week of the year. Its sole purpose is a reset. If you look back, my journals will be filled with notes, goals, dreams, and sketches from those trips that become watermarks for the year to come.

Why Dreams Matter

I had a dream in 2007 that was so clear. It is why you are here today.

Summer of 2007 was one of the hardest of my life. Your mom and I were ships passing in the night. She worked nights as a well-loved TV personality in one city, and I worked during the day in another, and we lived halfway in between. No kids, no thought of kids. I should also mention, we had very few deep friendships and little community. We had a garage full of stuff, but our hearts were pretty empty (and so was our checking account!). On the outside, I bet we looked pretty good, but on the inside we were a mess.

That summer, I had a dream—or more of a vision—that was filled with what we now know two decades later to be a direct foreshadowing of things to come. In that dream, I saw myself rescuing your mom from her work and life choices and the two of us walking past old brick buildings as we faced death across the street. In the end, we were surrounded by three older figures that said, "Thank you, we love you." >

There were a lot more personal details to that dream, all of which came true, but my point is: That dream gave me a vision for something I could not see on my own. It was something I could hold onto that felt like it was from God, something I constantly went back to when times were hard for your mom and me. That vision helped to keep me faithfully by your mom's side through all of life's turmoil—some self-inflicted and some that were just part of the human experience, such as cancer. And in the end, I still believe those three older figures were you, my children.

I've since gone on to have other dreams—some just craziness, but others as clear as a sunrise in my mind that gave me insights about an upcoming death or a person who needed help. The challenge becomes knowing which ones matter. All I can tell you is, like the truth, you will know it when you see it. Hold onto those dreams. Use them. Lean on them. One day you might find yourself in the middle of life's hardest moments and need that reminder to grasp onto.

"New ideas must use old buildings."

—Jane Jacobs

Old Buildings, New Ideas

In 2007, your mom and I were separated. Our marriage was a mess, and we needed a new dream. In 2009, we decided that our new dream was a hundred-year-old brick warehouse. We had been to Charleston, SC on a trip soon after renewing our vows and saw the beautiful, adaptive reuse projects in the port city: old buildings now filled with new life. Perfect? No. Rough in areas, new in others. Reborn with a new purpose.

We saw resurrection.

I still believe that to be true. I believe there is a desire in us all, deep in our DNA, to see resurrection. Sometimes, we are not even aware of it, but when spring arrives every year, you feel it. When you see the before and after photos of a makeover, an old car, or, in our world, forgotten buildings and homes—you feel it.

We felt it. That idea helped to save our marriage (along with a lot of hard work, counseling, and tears). It gave us something to dream about together. We went on to rebuild and restore dozens of homes and more >

than 150,000 square feet of our little Virginia community. It's work I am still doing today, because I believe in its power to change the mindset and landscape of our neighborhood and our collective community.

Old buildings do need new ideas in order for them to have new life and to become relevant. Often they have good bones, and if you can dream, and see something no one else can imagine, you can experience resurrection. It feels a lot like bringing heaven to earth.

Without being too heavy-handed on the metaphor, the same was and is true in marriage. It's hard work, but new life can be breathed into the broken spaces your hearts reside in. Will it ever be the same? No. But the repairs often make it stronger and have a beauty of their own.

There is a desire in us all,
deep in our DNA, to see resurrection.

1952 Chevy

When I was fifteen, I traded a cow for a truck. It was a 1952 Chevrolet pickup. It had come from an estate auction my parents spent a fall Saturday attending (they loved estate auctions). It was a roller. It did not run. There was not a piece of metal on that truck that was not covered in years of rust, but I loved it. I loved the idea and the romance of it. I would spend hours in my mind and on paper drawing it out, making lists of what was next and then flipping through old parts catalogs to create a shopping list.

Yes, I traded a cow for it. Technically, I kind of just gave Dad his cow back, but it was mine to choose. Dad gave us each a young calf; it was our responsibility to care for it, and then we could decide its fate. I swapped ol' Bessie for four kinda inflated tires and a teenage driving dream.

I learned how to do everything. I completely disassembled that truck and slowly put it back together. I did engine work, body work, all of it . . . and then I went away to college and left an unfinished project in my parents' barn.

Over the returning summers, I slowly saved enough money, used enough elbow grease, and won the favor of enough guys like my Uncle Kevin to help me finish the truck. When I finished the truck, I was twenty-one years old. It had taken six years. That final college summer of 2001, my brother and I drove it to work at Pipestem State Park, where we were horseback trail guides. It was a summer of stories, very few of which can make this book, but by the next spring, I had sold the truck. Six years of work gone, for enough cash to pay some student debt.

I still feel happy inside every time I see a 1949–1953 Chevy half-ton. Funny enough, unlike most guys who say, "I shouldn't have sold it," I feel the opposite. I'm fine with the fact that I sold it. It was about the journey for me. I learned the lesson of trading something for something else no one wanted and then having the vision to restore it bolt by bolt until the final product was a standing piece of my artwork. I figure we don't really get to keep things anyway; we are really just stewarding them. So the journey, process, and education of learning how to disassemble and reassemble a truck was a lesson much more valuable than the truck itself.

Field Trips

Everyone likes a field trip day at school. Permission slips are signed. Buses are boarded. Then there's a change in scenery and schedule. Take field trips as an adult too. Do it regularly. Find a reason to pick up a purchase on the road or visit a nearby city overnight. A day or two will do. A moment away forms a different view. Take your camera and your notepad because you'll bring home some inspiration if you're open to it.

P.S. Field trips also don't take much planning. They are more laid-back. Often they are within driving distance. Don't forget to pack snacks. . . .

Big Ideas, Bite-Size Chunks

There is no easy way to say this: Small minds dream small, and you do not have small minds. You are gonna have big ideas. Chase them fearlessly. Don't let the size scare you. Don't let the cost scare you. Don't freeze up when you realize the time investment. Every large creative project is made of smaller creative chunks. Learn to see the end product in your mind, and then start to see the chunks. Eat the elephant one bite at a time. Write them all down, organize them into buckets, and take on one at a time.

The secret is to focus on one chunk at a time. Just make sure you love the elephant you're about to eat.

If the Client Wants It Pink, Make It Pink

I was twenty-two years old driving a red Firebird, blasting Jimmy Eat World and DMX on a burned CD. I was headed to NY/NJ for my first post-grad job. I looked like a mix of Vanilla Ice and a kid who fell into a retro jersey three times too big for him. My first boss out of college was a saucy Italian lady, Grace. She was a no-bullshit industry veteran who could cut through the design of a merchandising display faster than anyone I had ever seen. Her pad, pen, and fingers on the keyboard danced in perfect rhythm as she made design after design come to life on her huge Mac screens. She taught me so much about design and efficiency and how to survive the city, but she also taught me the most important lesson I learned as a creative professional:

If the client wants it pink, you make it pink.

What that meant was: If this were your own art, if this were your own store, you could do whatever your little backstreet-boy-looking heart desires, but you are being paid to create something here. It's a transaction. Be creative. Make something cool, but if they want to make it pink, make it pink.

That approach has served me, and others on my creative teams, well over the years. When I realized most of what I create is about solving the client's problem, I found freedom in helping. As a creative, when it comes to helping, let the client tell you what they need.

I can already hear the question: "But what if they don't know what they need?" I would argue that they do, and it's your job to ask great questions. There will be a day when someone asks you to scrap the art or writing you stayed up all-night working on to deliver only to hear they want something different. Or maybe they just want some subtle changes to the work you have done. Don't get butthurt by it. Ask better questions. Write the answers down, and leave knowing that making it pink is the way to go in order to get where you want to be.

"Bring Me a Rock" Game

Ah, the old "bring me a rock" game. Not this rock, a different rock. . . . It's a game you play with children to keep them busy. When it's played with you as a creative person in an agency or client-side setting, it is exhausting. Whether it's from a creative director or a client, for a creative, it feels like having your tires stuck in the sand—you are going nowhere.

Don't play the game.

Play a different game by asking better questions, writing down the answers, and returning to the design table with a solution that solves the problem using the answers provided. Repeat the answers back to the other party as you show them the work. Remind them of their own answers at the time. Show them the new rock they asked for.

And if the other party wants to continue the game? Fine, charge more.

Go for a Walk or Take a Shower

Creatively, you will get stuck.

It happens. It's not a block as much as a blank. Just a damn mental void. When that happens, push away from your desk and go take a walk or a shower. Get some sun or some water on your skin. I swear either will work. If you're really jammed up on the problem, do both—just make sure they are in that order.

Happiness When You Wake Up

The sooner you realize that you're the only one concerned about your happiness when you wake up, the quicker you will make choices.

Zippering My Wiener

When I was four years old, I refused to wear underwear.

The consequence was a careless "zipppp" of my Rustler jeans right into my little man bits. And it was stuck! Think *Something About Mary*-style—but I'm four.

Ouch.

It became a family event. My parents, at a loss for how to perform this denim surgery, called my grandparents, and my uncle showed up too. Here I am laying in the bed with everyone staring at my junk, in distress, and my uncle says, "I guess we'll have to cut it off."

I lost my mind. Traumatic.

What he meant was the zipper.

I was freed by a pair of needle nose pliers and some kitchen scissors, with just a few zipper marks on my man parts.

After that event, I drove my mom crazy with extra laundry. For years I rocked two layers of underwear, believing the extra layer would protect me from a second circumcision! It worked until I realized how to handle the hardware (on both ends).

Life is like that: Sometimes it takes a painful moment to figure out how to prevent the same hurt from happening again. What I'm saying is, protect your private parts—even if it means wearing two pairs of tighty-whities for a while.

Most of Your Work Will Be Forgotten

If you're a creative—a designer, photographer, writer, or painter—most of your work will end up in the trash.

For more than twenty years, I did design work for big, big footwear brands and stores. I designed everything from print to digital. I made videos, music, websites, and everything in between, and none of it is still in use. Even the stuff that won awards only lives on a backup drive somewhere today. The unfortunate truth for creatives is that most work will end up dying in someone's inbox, or else, after the campaign is over, it will go in the trash.

Use that as motivation. When it comes to creative work for hire, understand that it will have a lifespan—even brand logos change over time—and because of that, there is opportunity to do more! Evolve as a maker. Try new things, push yourself, go in a direction and then shift. Just know that over time, your work will evolve with you. As a young creative, get reps, as many as possible. Those reps will help you form creative muscle memory, which will give you quick recall when completing a project well.

There may come a time when your work starts to become more semi-permanent. Maybe it's a larger painting on a building, maybe it's the building itself, or maybe your beautiful words are read by generations. Do it all with the understanding that most people will never understand the amount of work you've done to get here, and for each person, it will be new the first time they encounter your work. So keep creating. Be the kind of people who are always putting energy back on the grid, not just gluttonously absorbing the work of others without offering something in return.

Be the kind of people who are always putting energy back on the grid, not just gluttonously absorbing the work of others without offering something in return.

Small Gems

Be a small gems person. It's never the big, over-the-top, grand things that will make the greatest impact or stick with you. It's often a little piece of sea glass, a handful of pink sand, or a photograph that will spark your heart and mind.

The last trip your mom and I took was for our twentieth anniversary to the Bahamas with Brandon and Brittany. We went all out. We did it up! We booked a big ocean-front room at an ultra luxurious hotel/casino overlooking nothing but miles and miles of crystal blue waters.

But your mom knew she was dying. She passed away about sixty days after this trip. Besides trips to the doctor's office, this would be the last journey we would experience together.

Looking back now, I know she was exhausted; she slept a lot, but to her credit, she did her best to keep up. She rallied strength in her failing body, and we did as much as she could. She even rode waterslides with us that week! BTW, your mom hated waterslides—something about being in the water with millions of strands of DNA that are not yours. This was proof she was really sick. She had lost her breasts the previous year and hated being in a bathing suit too. At some point she said, "I don't give a damn anymore." I loved her for that. She was swelling daily from fluid retention, and her liver was not processing nutrients to help her body or mind.

Late one night on the trip, I was able to convince her (and Brittany of course) to take a small plane (gosh, they hated small planes—like a-cat-on-a-leash hated small planes) to Harbour Island, a remote spot in the Bahamas known by those who love *Coastal Living* but visited by few. Its charm, patina, and almost carefree, worn-in nature make every photo feel ideal.

We boarded the small plane, hopped a couple of islands, and found ourselves standing outside a run-down pink shack (the control tower) before hopping into a sketchy van for the three-minute ride to the docks. >

At the docks, we boarded a well-worn vessel from the 1960s along with the working locals, stacks of produce, and tools. I sat in the back near the two outboard Yamaha 150s, soaking in the smells of gasoline and seawater. As they fired up and turned into the surf, I found myself in a catatonic state. The sounds and smells of these two engines, the water, and the sun, they took me to a place of freedom. It felt familiar and wild at the same time. There's a beautiful blend of rhythm and scent on boats like this, plus the adrenaline that comes with gliding across the open water.

Side note:
Find your outboard engines, the sounds and spaces that clear your mind. When these sights and sounds are coupled with smell—the strongest sense for recall—you will be able to bring back beautiful memories.

As we docked at Harbour Island, the four of us climbed into an old gasoline powered golf cart to cruise around the island. The smallness of the place sat in such contrast to the massive four-diamond resort/casino we had just come from. The chickens in the street, the late open of the bakery, the pace of the people on the street. All well worn. All laid back. All made beautiful with time and patina.

As we wove our way out toward the beach in the cart, tiny hotels began to peek out from behind the foliage. Small boutique stays, perfectly imperfect worn whites and greens, the picture of coastal carefree—as if they had grown there, and were never changed. No large stone entrances, no million-dollar cars out front, no flash and glam—a place where the only clock was the sun and the changing of the tides. It was heaven.

I should mention that we were alone on the beach for miles. Miles and miles of pink sand and screensaver-esque blue water in front of us—the edge of the earth.

It wasn't the *big* of the day, it was the small. It wasn't the perfect, it was actually the imperfect that made the biggest impression. Time, nature, and honest modesty had made these perfect little gems. Those types of gems are the perfect size to carry in your mind and heart.

See With Your Mind (and Your Heart)

Learn to see with your mind. Be able to let yourself envision the shape, space, and position of the art you are about to endeavor to create. After years of working in design, photography, and building in physical spaces, it comes easily to me, but when you first get started as a creative, often the hardest part is just that: getting started. There will be times, creatively, throughout your career when it's easy to see the end product. It's easy to take the perfect photo, do the right design layout, or build the ideal space. In the beginning, not so much. You have not learned to flex that muscle quite yet. It will take time, but often the more you do it, the faster it will come.

Learn to sit quietly and stare (or sometimes close your eyes) at the blank wall, the canvas, or the old building. Start to see it taking shape. As you do, make a quick sketch or a note to yourself. Begin to lock it away.

Now here is when it gets real: Can you "feel" it yet? Can you almost touch the finished product in your mind? Can you see the people in the space? Can you feel the warmth of the light and the reflections in the image? Think about all of these *before* you actually create.

Here is why this is important: You are about to move from nothing—a blank screen, blank canvas, empty memory card, or old dilapidated building—into beginning the work of creating. While you need to see it for yourself, you also need to "feel" it to communicate your vision to others along the way. As you pitch the campaign, as you instruct your subjects on where/how to stand/look, as you share your vision with the bank or partners for funding . . . you have to "feel" it in order for it to be real and meaningful when you communicate it to those around you. >

. ..clearly communicate the idea and vision. But don't overcomplicate it. Distill it down. Fill it with meaning. Don't over-explain—when you are explaining, you are losing.

But why is that important? Because it will be a collective work/project/campaign that requires buy-in or partnership from those around you. And to get others on board with your vision that does not exist yet, you must be able to share it with them in such a way that it feels real already.

Don't skip this part. You will need to get others on board.

You will need to be able to clearly communicate the idea and vision. But don't overcomplicate it. Distill it down. Fill it with meaning. Don't over-explain—when you are explaining, you are losing.

The rub comes when they "just don't get it" and completely miss your vision. Sometimes it's a lack of creativity or willingness on their part, but what about your part? Did you communicate the invisible idea with feeling and emotion that brought it to life for them? Before you blame someone else for not understanding your creative direction, make certain that you have taken the time to "feel" it. Make sure you believe it first, and then share it.

Here is the risk: They might hate it.

Your boss might hate the direction, your clients might dislike the photo idea, or the city may not be ready for the renovation ideas you are proposing. That will happen, and when it does, write it down. Take note of the "NO," but the vast majority of the time, you will find that if you can "pitch" your vision with genuine feeling, the audience will respond positively to it.

You might call this selling the art.

Being a Blue-Ribbon Hog Caller

When I was a kid, my room was filled with those ten-inch-tall sparkly gold trophies. Sports, slot cars, Bible bowls . . . but the most memorable trophy I can recall had a pig on it. When I was seven, I won the West Virginia State Fair hog-calling contest for kids. No lie. I'm not sure what that says about me as a young, fat kid, but I just think you need to know that I can bring home the bacon.

I am not an expert on any of the following, but rather a practitioner. I've found that the heart drives all things, so who you choose as friends, who you marry, and the community you spend your life connected to will have a huge impact on every other aspect of your life.

Write this down, and underline it:

You will become who you spend your time with. Choose people who cheer for you, people who show up, and people who tell the truth.

Oh, and be curious, not judgmental. To be a good friend or partner takes being truly interested in the other person—trying to understand them, what makes them tick. Your mom was great at this: She loved asking people about themselves. What you'll find is that most people are happy to talk about themselves if you just ask.

I know it's corny, but having great people around you will make you feel like the richest person in the world. On the other hand, if the relationships around you are drama-filled, you will be constantly exhausted by the additional weight you will carry.

Do Drugs With Friends

The best drugs are taken in sweaty doses with friends. Do it early in the day too. The best cocktail is a workout that requires almost, just almost, more than you had to give. Follow it up with a quick breather and then a good cup of coffee together.

There is something special about sweating side-by-side and then sitting face-to-face.

I've done this for years with rotating groups of men called my "Warrior" groups. We meet around 5 a.m., bust some ass together, and then sit and unpack things in a vulnerable way that we would not in other circles. Men's Bible studies were always too soft. Most of the guys in those groups are snacks when the dinosaurs return to roam the earth. Kind? Sure. Do I trust them? Hell no. So we started these groups years ago to find men we could trust. We found that forty-five minutes of exercise and forty-five minutes of deep conversation satisfied our souls once a week better than any other circle we had sat in.

So find a group of folks you can work alongside, push, and then listen to. I promise that when you leave those mornings, it's a high like you won't find anywhere else.

Keep Your Promises,
Even When It Costs You Something

It will. Keeping your promises will always cost you something. Time, money, energy—yes, those and more.

Be the kind of person who keeps their promises. You will find that this simple habit will make you so rare in life and love.

I kept my promises to your mom for more than twenty years. I promised to be faithful to her alone. To care for her in sickness and in health. Until death. I did just that. Through her crazy career in TV, through the pain of her deep wounds and depression, through cancer . . . fucking cancer . . . I kept my promises to her through the very moments of wrapping her up into the sheets and laying her in the body bag on a gurney. I placed her into the hearse.

Until death.

Keep your promises. At the end of each day, you will be able to stand straight, stare into the eyes of any audience, and know with a clear conscience that you did it with honor. It won't be easy, but trust me: The clarity of your heart and mind afterward will be worth it.

On the flip side: In your life you will have people who don't keep their promises, to you or your community. In marriages, in business, in friendships. I would highly advise you: Do not continue to give them your time or mental space. They will only continue a pattern of taking without giving, canceling last minute, and never paying their share. Spend your energy with people who keep their word.

Be the kind of person who keeps their promises. You will find that this simple habit will make you so rare in life and love.

Wear Your Scars on the Front

There is an old story about Alexander the Great. Boiled down, it goes something like this: Long war, men are tired, ready to return home, big enemy ahead, and morale is low. Alex comes out in front of the team and says, "Hey boys, haven't I always been with you?" A-Money tears off his clothes and says, "See my scars, my battle wounds, they are all on the front—there are none on my back." And the crowd goes wild. . . . The rest is literally history, but in greater detail.

Here is my point: Face your battles head-on. Don't turn your back and run.

I'm covered in scars. A lot of them are from my own stupidity, and all of our scars tell a story.

Your mom and your grandmothers carried all of their scars on the front too. Each of them had her breasts removed because of cancer. Parts of their physical person that often defined their womanhood, their sexuality, or feminity—were lost to a battle with their bodies. While they covered the losses daily with clothing, each of those women had to see the results of those wars every day in the mirror. They faced it daily. They didn't run. They stared it down—head-on and chest out.

Don't run. Bare your scars on the front. It will remind you and the rest of the world, "I do not run away from a fight." There is honor in those marks.

Bare your scars on the front.
It will remind you and the rest of the world,
"I do not run away from a fight."

There is honor in those marks.

I'm Covered in Scars

I learned early on the farm that most wounds just need peroxide and a butterfly bandage (or bandages). I have scars to prove it! Most of these wounds healed, and their marks have little impact on my daily life, but the memory of how stupid I was to get them makes me a more alert father. I've shot myself with an arrow (go ahead, try to figure out that riddle), fallen through metal filing cabinets, seared my forearms on go-kart mufflers, ripped open my hands on barbed wire, split open my chin and forehead multiple times, and even found a way to cut my foot in half with a rope. All true. BTW, the last one did require more than a butterfly bandage.

Then there are the ones you volunteered for. I have the busted knuckles and broken fingers of a young man who liked to punch other young men on accident and on purpose. My headaches and chipped teeth remind me that I used to run into other humans with a pretty basic football helmet for fun. I've always enjoyed the risk and reward that come with contact. I chose those wounds, so I'm good with the cost.

It's the wounds we don't choose that hurt the worst. Finding healing and making sense of the pain you didn't sign up for will always be the hardest—but you've got two options. You can curl up, ignore it, and let it get infected, or you can choose to try and clean it out as best you can so you can start to heal. Trust me, it's painful up front but worth it in the end.

Steal Sunrises

If you want to win, get up early or stay up late. The downside to staying up late is that nothing good happens after midnight. So that leaves getting up early. It might come naturally, but to most, it won't, which is the secret. Yeah, at first, it will suck, but train yourself to do it and you will create the extra margin that your workouts, spirit, and work require.

Listen, your family won't care what time you get up, but they will care what time you get home.

Steal sunrises. Don't steal time from them.

Showing up is about two things:
being consistent and being present.
When you bury me, this is what I want
written on my grave: *He Showed Up.*

Show Up

Showing up is about two things: being consistent and being present. Both, done over a long period of time, will compound into valued friendships and a reputation that is better than gold.

Along the lines of keeping your promises, just showing up for people will make you rare. Mark my words: Watch your life/relationships for a decade, and take note of who is still standing with you. Who made their presence known when moving day or death came. I promise you the list will be very short.

Why? Why is simply showing up so hard? Because it requires sacrifice. It is one of those characteristics—like telling the truth or keeping your word—that will cost you something. Often, the price is your time and probably your comfort. Most of the time, showing up means work—most of it unpaid when it comes to friends or family! But show up.

Yes, it's good to show up at all the important stuff that you are invited to—weddings, birthdays, graduations, etc.—but showing up for the things that no one invites you to is the secret. Show up when a friend's brother dies and he is stuck with the task of moving his stuff. Show up when your sister needs to go to the cancer center. Show up when your friend loses her keys in the yard and needs a ride. Show up when your kids have kids, and be the grandparents you both need.

When you bury me, this is what I want written on my grave: *He Showed Up.*

The reason fear and love cannot exist together is that if you are afraid, you will never really commit to love.

When You Fear, You Can't Love

If you are afraid of losing something, you will squeeze it so tightly that your grip will kill it. Fear and love can't exist together, just like safety and courage don't mix.

When it comes to changing your job, starting a business, moving across the country, or even having kids, you will freeze at the intersection of your decisions. I highly encourage you to push past it and choose the unknown, because you will only regret the things you don't do in life.

But when it comes to love . . . oh boy, love . . . choosing to live open-handed is scary as shit.

After you live through abuse, maybe a couple of affairs, and the deep hurts of relationships, you will be so afraid to live with a loose grip on love. I've often viewed romantic love like a small beautiful bird in my hand. If you squeeze, you will kill that little thing. But if you live with an open hand, you run the risk of the love bird flying away. . . . That's where courage comes in. If the bird flies away and returns, you know it's real, but if you open your hand to love and the bird takes flight, never to return, you are better off.

The reason fear and love cannot exist together is that you will hedge on one or the other. If you are afraid, you will never really commit to love, and the kind of commitment that allows complete freedom within your agreed-upon boundaries creates a level of trust like you have never felt before.

¡ES UN GUSTO!
Make a Way for Others

"It's a joy."

That should be your response when someone thanks you for your help.

Serving others should be your joy.

Leadership should mean service, not reward.
Love should mean giving, not taking.

You will find more meaning in the giving. You will find that making a way for others will yield a greater return than saving it all for yourself.

Hard truth: You will get burned. You will get used. You will find yourself on the short end of the deal, and if you let yourself, you will grow bitter and angry about it. Those moments will steal from your peace and make you cynical, and your battle will be to not let them.

You will learn the patterns and behaviors of users and narcissists. You will learn what unhealthy and evil people look like. Separate yourself from those people and move on.

You may not see the fruits of your investments in others very quickly. Just like with your children—you are planting trees, and you may never sit in their shade. It's a long-term investment.

Leadership should mean service,
not reward.

Love should mean giving,
not taking.

Trading in Bernard

Once, I traded a dog for a better dog. I was five. We had a purebred beagle named Bernard. He was supposed to be a good hunting dog. I remember B was cute, but he was scared of everything. He whined a lot and would hide behind your leg. Definitely not the hunting hound he was billed to be.

One day, a curly-tailed mutt, a black Elkhound/lab mix with a white stripe on her chest, showed up at my grandparents' house. Mamaw took in the stray with butter-based table scraps, and when we came over to play, I fell in love with "Oreo."

I wanted to take Oreo home, so I petitioned Dad for another dog.

Nope. You have a dog.

But I like this dog better. *Nope.*

Bernard needs a buddy. *Nope.*

You want that dog? You would have to get rid of Bernard, and you don't want to do that, do you?

Yep. I do.

I don't think he thought I was serious. I definitely don't think Bernard thought any of us were serious.

Until Papaw, the man wanting to be rid of the stray dog at his house, showed up the next Saturday in his little white pickup about to do a dog swap.

The deal was done, and I vividly remember watching Papaw drive away with Bernard staring out the passenger window on his way to a new home.

You know what, that turned out to be one of the best dog deals of a kid's lifetime. Oreo became our sidekick. Our curly-tailed protector. She went everywhere we went for more than a decade, mostly in the back of Dad's 1968 Chevy "Old Red." Most of my childhood memories of a dog involve Oreo, and had I never called Dad's dog bluff, I would have missed a boy's best friend. And when it comes to most things, mutts are better than purebreds any day.

Don't Explain Suffering

Don't try to explain away suffering in an attempt to comfort friends or family. Truth is, you are trying to round the edges off a sharp surface so you feel better yourself. Seeing someone suffer or even hearing of their suffering is hard. But remember, the person going through it is living in that reality daily. Don't attempt to speak for God. Don't attempt to know the reason why it has happened. Lastly, don't try to make them feel better with common phrases or sayings.

"I am hurting with you. I love you. I'll bring over dinner" is all you need to say. Then you do. Show up with dinner and a hug. Keep your mouth closed and your arms and ears open. Feel free to ask questions, but don't have answers.

Allow yourself to feel their hurt. Allow their suffering to have meaning. One of my favorite guidepost books has been *Man's Search for Meaning* by Viktor Frankl, in which he teaches that we find meaning in three areas of life: love, work, and suffering.

Don't shy away from the truth of the pain. Don't let yourself go numb.

If you do not demand peace from love,
then you are accepting a less-than-true
form. Do not accept anything less.

What to Demand From Love

People will often quip that love is free. False. Love comes with a price. For it to be real and true, love will demand something more of you, so you must in turn demand something of it. Your demands of love should be: faithfulness, honesty, and care that comes with deep commitment. Anything less is just affection.

True love brings peace. That peace comes from resting in the confidence that your partner, friend, or family member will be there tomorrow. That their intent is positive. That any harm done was not caused by malice, but rather just carelessness, and it will be corrected. If you do not demand peace from love, then you are accepting a less-than-true form. Do not accept anything less. In return, love will bring warmth and light to your home each morning. It will bring a foundation for the days of hard things. It will bring rest each night, knowing that the sun will rise tomorrow, and together you will find a way forward.

And on that final day—the day your loved one breathes a final deep sigh, the day everyone fears—you will stand again, steady and sure of love.

Ok, but what's the cost, you ask?

The cost is paid in daily deposits, not grand gestures. Those deposits are made best in a currency that is consistently backed by your presence—again, showing up. Bring joy and words of affirmation to your relationships. It will cost you choosing to show up and do the hard things for one another over, and over, and over again. It will cost you lots of grace—for both parties involved. Love will never be a passive investment. Your returns will be directly related to the effort you put in, and it is because of that demand the returns reflect the same—faithfulness, honesty, and care.

The Magnet & the Sparks

You will feel it. A powerful draw. It will feel like a magnet pulling you in, connecting you. It will be so strong of a pull that it's clear: This is not mere attraction, but rather a perfect pairing. A coupling together of two forces. It is love on a deeper level.

In your lifetime, you are going to "love" and be loved by so many. I know it. Our clan is built for connection. You will have connections with family, with friends, and of course hopefully in romance, but that magnetic connection you can feel with another person will be rare in your lifetime. It may come early in life, it may come later . . . to be candid, for some, it may never come at all. The wrestling lies in being healthy enough to sense it, the vibration, and then attempting to control the sparks that fly as these beautiful metallic objects smash against each other.

Sparks, when not contained, equal fire. Those flames are sometimes good, sometimes bad.

As a father, I don't want you to get burned. I don't want you to bear the scars of hurt. As a peer, what I will tell you is to let it burn. Fire is fire. It will try what is true. It will prove what is real. If your relationship is shallow, the flame will fizzle fast. If it's authentic, it will continue to burn; it will have to be tended, but it will be a burning that will never go out. Both of these have risks. Becoming a burn victim of love will leave scarring that is hardly ever repaired. It will feel like giving away all of yourself only to have it returned burnt, charred, with the residue of hurt all over it. Your body, heart, finances, and family will all pay the price.

Remember, you too have a responsibility: Don't start a fire that you are not willing to put out. Set your non-negotiables for relationships. Do not waver on them. And when you make the wrong call in love, give yourself grace. Repair your wounds. Move forward again.

In my own life, what I've found true about fire is that it is mesmerizing. It changes shapes. It creates beauty. It's a fine line between enjoyment and fear, usefulness and destruction. But I will always choose to live with it, rather than fear the burn.

Sparks, when not contained,
equal fire. Those flames are
sometimes good, sometimes bad...
Don't start a fire that you are not
willing to put out.

Mind the Gap

When your mom died, my phone exploded. It took days to follow up on all the texts, messages, and phone calls.

And then there was the next day, and the next, and a year later there was a gap. That gap is the space between the current moment and your last communication with someone—in today's world, a relational gap that was reflected visually in my text messages.

As I look back at the gaps between today and those messages of sympathy after her death in 2023, it is a visual representation of relationships. For some relationships that space is fine, even wanted—but be mindful of the gap. It shows you just how close or important your relationship is to that person. And, sometimes, you can become so concerned about how you "think" people will feel or perceive you, or even with the idea that they are thinking heavily or often about your situation. Truth is, they are not. The gap proves it.

Struggling Together

Fact: If you are a human, there will be struggle.

Key: Pick who you want to struggle alongside you.

How to Pick: Choose a person you could go to war with. Trust, clarity, and creativity should be among the top attributes of your partner. Choose well, not often.

FAITH + DEATH

Truth is, your faith will be deeply personal. And while I have raised you in a home that believes in a Creator God, and while we pray grace of gratitude over each meal together, I cannot give you the certainties of religion that I grew up being told were the only way.

Your mom and I were both products of families who were/are heavily involved in the local Christian churches. There are lots of labels we could attach here, but just know that we were required to be at church every time someone unlocked the doors. Your mom wrestled with the faith of her youth during the entirety of our marriage. She had been through so many hard things in her own life and saw the harm the church did to her family. When cancer struck our family multiple times before her own, your grandmothers and grandfather, we continued to pray and pray for healing. After treatments and surgeries, healing came for your grandparents...

It did not for her. I'm so sorry.

I can understand how this immediately brings so many questions to the forefront for you. I have struggled with many of them too. All I can tell you is that we have brains the size of red solo cups, and filling them with all we can of God still leaves an ocean full of mysteries.

Your faith will grow and shrink in your lifetime. Make it your own. Ask questions. Be curious. Pray prayers of thanks. Scream out in times of need. **Find community where it's safe to not be certain**—the kind of place where people are always looking to grow and learn more about their Creator and the foundations of the faith.

Today, I still believe we were uniquely created by a God who wove the universe together in ways we can never fully know, but the ways of Jesus lead us closer to that understanding. I'm okay with never having the answers for you, but I pray your journey leads you to find ways to bring more Kingdom to Earth and gives you hope and a home in the times when you feel lost.

Avoid the Fish People

People tell you exactly who they are. Often, those tells come in the form of symbols and bumper stickers. In my experience, I've found that the people loudest about Jesus through these icons are often the least likely to follow the Way. It's as though the adoption of the symbol is enough. It makes them part of a club in their minds, when in truth, our faith should be way less about what we say (or post) and way more about what we do: feed the poor, care for orphans and widows, love all of our neighbors as ourselves—do the work to bring more Kingdom to earth.

Wrestling the Ocean (Surrender at Sea)

The beautiful thing about prayer is that you are completely free to pray for whatever you like. I grew up in a place that taught that God always answered! Always. That God always responded with a YES, NO, or WAIT. That's a funny way of speaking for God, and I don't recall ever clearly hearing any of those three answers after more than four decades of faith.

What I've learned is to pray with honor and thanks. I ask for the Kingdom to come to Earth. I say thank you for our daily bread. And I ask God to forgive us for the way we have harmed others. That's it! I've stopped asking for things. Why? Because I do not believe that's the way the universe is wired. I do believe you can create or manifest things by looking for them or doing the work, but that's another conversation. But when it comes to bags of money or healing from cancer . . . neither one of those is on the list of things to pray for. Pray for peace. Pray for comfort. Say thank you, often. But as for "the prayers of a righteous man," don't let yourself get lost in that "name it and claim it" perspective.

Your mom once said, "Everyone wants me to spiritualize my cancer. I don't believe that is true. I believe this is just unfortunately part of being human and through this, I will learn something about myself, and if I'm lucky I will learn something about God." I know she was spot-on. >

After she died, I didn't pray for months. It felt like a waste of energy after praying the same prayers for over four years. After thousands and thousands of people had prayed those same prayers. Listen, I'm not the most "righteous" of individuals, but someone in those thousands of people faithfully praying (I'll start with Rachel) absolutely was worthy of the label "righteous" . . . and yet, no healing like I was promised by family and "Bible-believing" church folk happened.

So why pray?

It was 5 a.m. on the beach in Wilmington. It was a cold, rainy November morning. A dark, blue sky over a roaring ocean. I felt the draw to get in. So I did, with the mindset of wrestling. I was in just five or six feet of water, thrashing around in the foam, when it hit me.

The ocean doesn't care that I'm there. In fact, all of my wrestling doesn't even create a ripple in the ocean. The ocean is undefeated. It has swallowed up people and ships much greater than me. It was then that I realized it was just about surrender. My prayer was simply, "I surrender. I get it, God: You, like the ocean you created, are bigger than me. It's not my place to ask for or demand anything. It's merely my place to surrender. I don't understand your bigness, just like I cannot fathom the depths of this sea. I won't be asking for anything. I understand my place. Thank you."

And so I swam back out of the waves and collapsed on the beach. My wrestling was over. I had lost, but I had also won a new perspective. God is bigger than you. Don't make a smaller version of God in your image (the poems of Genesis remind us that it's the other way around). Embrace the mystery. Stop fighting the current and say thank you.

"Concerns"

The fears others have for your life are most often just judgments repackaged as concerns—made from positions where they have the luxury of returning home to the safety of their same life/spouse/ career. So, if you really want to create something new and beautiful, don't let the fears of others become your own.

How to Cook a Bunny

When I was a little boy, my father went rabbit hunting on a fall Saturday. He bagged a couple of hares and brought them home for my mother to prepare. My mom, an army-brat, world-traveled, officer's-club daughter, immediately called my Mamaw (her mother-in-law).

"Charlotte, how do you cook a bunny?" asked my mom.

"Sweetie, the first thing you do is don't call it a bunny," shared Mamaw.

When something is a difficult truth, don't try to be too sweet about it. Be kind, but be true. Often, naming the hard thing for exactly what it is takes away some of its power. Be direct. Call the thing what it is.

We ate rabbit pretty often after that.

Please Don't Lay Hands on Me

I grew up in a faith tradition that taught, when someone was sick, the elders of the church should lay hands on the afflicted and pray prayers of healing. And as they were righteous people, those prayers would be heard and the person healed. Beautiful idea. I get it. And while I do think it's a beautiful picture of community and caring, I've mostly found the opposite to be true.

Often, when someone lays hands on you to pray over you, it starts with good intentions, but the topic turns in milliseconds to their personal fear of death, a need for authority, and some misaligned theology on miraculous healings. Oh, and my favorite: blaming it on the "ol' Sayton"—the devil himself. As the moments pass, the culmination leaves the prayed-for feeling a sense of "What the heck was that?"

I was told that the prayers of the righteous would heal. Do I count? Ha, probably not on days that end in Y, but I can be 100% sure of the righteousness of Nana and thousands of others like her who prayed over your mom. Why didn't that work? If that's all it takes, why didn't the righteous prayers of thousands save your mom's life and miraculously heal her fully cancer-engulfed liver?

Because that's not how it works. >

Often, when someone lays hands on you to pray over you, it starts with good intentions, but the topic turns in milliseconds to their personal fear of death...and some misaligned theology

———

There are miracles. There are miraculous healings. There are people prayed over that seemingly come back from the doorstep of death itself. I've been a witness to it. But the randomness of those healings cannot be ascribed to the presence or absence of righteous prayer. That is a path of virtue paved by human perspectives. Healings like that are simply unexplainable. They are a byproduct of a spiritual and a physical world colliding in a space we do not fully understand.

Should we lose hope? Should we stop praying for the sick? Should we stop asking God to heal our loved ones? If such prayer is honest and true to you, sure, go for it. The act of prayer itself often brings peace to the prayer(er?). I do still believe God works in the mystery of creation; we just truly don't know how it all works. Pray for your loved one's peace and comfort. Pray for their blessing and joy in a dark time. Pray they find rest. But for heaven's sake, do not bring a "faith healer" to their home. Don't ask them to come up front in a church setting. Don't tell them they are being afflicted by a demon. Don't tell them to repent in order to be healed. Oh, and in the future, if I am the sick one: Keep your hands off of me! The only hands I want on me are those of the ones I love, wrapped firmly around me in an embrace.

"I'm Good, You Go."

While we forget the details of most conversations, there are a few short phrases people will always remember in your voice.

The last couple of years of your mom's life had her on the sofa, on the bed, or in the chair in the corner. Resting. Trying to get better. It required more of me inside the home, caring for everyone's needs. Caring for her physically and emotionally was a daily job, all while parenting three kids. There were times when things needed to be done outside or away from the house, and she could tell I was chomping at the bit to get going. Often she would muster her strength, sit up, and say, "I'm good, you go."

One day, after she died, I was working outside our little circa-1895 office downtown when I heard her voice whisper that phrase again to me: "I'm good, you go." It bounced around in my head. I had heard her say it several times, but it meant something much deeper this time: "I'm good . . . for the first time in a long stretch, I'm good, really good. You go. You got this."

I have those words tattooed on my right arm.

My point is this: When you die, there will be a few phrases your people remember over time. If you say them often while you are alive, they will hear them after you're gone. Make your words count. Make them verbs.

Parenting Alone

If you ever find yourself as a single parent, know this: You can do it, but it is not for the weak. It may be one of life's hardest tasks to perform well alone, for the simple reason that your children will always be on your mind. The safety, security, and relief that come from having a partner in parenting are never fully replaced by babysitting, daycare, or even other family. Something about a partner holding down the fort while you tie up a loose end gives you a sense of peace to focus on the task at hand, but even with childcare, as a single parent, your mind is never fully at rest.

Single parents do not get a fair shake. We do not fairly assess or judge their situations and the effort required to do the task solo. Being a single parent is about survival. There is very little room for creativity. And any margin left for creativity is often gobbled up by daily tasks or pure exhaustion.

Being a single parent can also happen in a home with two people. We all know situations where one of the partners is always "at work" and the other carries the load, or a divorce causes a split and one of the partners is absent or unstable.

It can also happen with illness. In the last two years of your mom's life, when the cancer came back, I often found myself feeling like a single parent. I quit my full-time job to be more flexible for her and the three of you. I got you up for school in the mornings and rushed home early in the afternoon to get you off the bus. I transported you to and from school and friends' houses often because your mom was recovering from a surgery or chemo or she was just too tired. Homework and bedtimes . . . were most often handed to me while she was on the sofa or in the recliner, and then I would come back down to clean up and try to wrap up while she went to bed early. Even simple tasks like lifting Emmanuel in and out of his crib were too much for her at times.

She was present. She loved to snuggle with you in those days. She still loved to laugh with you and make fun of something ridiculous you were all spun up about. She was doing the best she could. I know that, and yet I still felt like a single parent.

My greatest fear when I thought about her dying was the idea of parenting you alone. I could not see how I would raise these two very creative but dramatic teenage girls and a toddler by myself. I was scared. I was also in training, and I didn't know it.

Yes, we have had the joy of great friends who are closer than family. (In fact, most days our home has looked like an episode of *Fuller House* in this first year.) Yes, your Nana & Poppop dug in even more . . . but in reality, it has just been me after trips unpacking you and getting you to bed. It's been me in your parent-teacher meetings making the best choices I can for your futures. It's been me on the rides to school trying to coach you up for the day. It's been me trying to direct your path as a single dad. Band-aids, bathtime, and buttermilk pancakes. Me.

Easy? No. Hard? Hell yes. Worth it? One thousand percent. Through my loving you and creating a safe place for you to grow, we will always honor your mom. Scared? No more. Humbled? Daily.

Learning to Say "I'm Sorry"

A proper apology does not have a "but," and it always begins with "I."

Learn to say "I'm sorry" to your friends, your spouse, and your kids as quickly as you can. Own it. Ask for their forgiveness. You're not responsible for their response, but you are responsible for making the first move toward healing with the simple bid of "I am sorry, forgive me for _____."

Sure, the big life goal is to stop hurting others completely so you never have to say it again, but the unfortunate truth is that all relationships, even the closest, will have harmful moments or unmet expectations—that you are responsible for. The secret is to sense that harm and take swift action toward helping your relationship mend. Healed scar tissue is stronger anyway.

Pursuit > Perfection

Don't let the need to get it exactly right stop you from making the attempt. In work or life, the pursuit of anything—designing, eating healthier, creating something beautiful, lifting more weight, or running further—will never be perfect, but in the pursuit of doing it well, you will grow and learn.

So many people in your life will never start because they fear failing or not doing it well. Blow right past those people and do the dang thing, even if it's wrong, messy, or not perfect; the pursuit will lead you to a place of learning and growth.

The goal: to keep your hands calloused and your heart soft.

The same is true in your relationship with God. Dig in. Read. Pray. Love your neighbor as yourself. But do not let the rigors of religion hold you in a place of fear because you "did not do it right." It is actually in the "doing" that you do it exactly right. Find a rhythm to your prayers, make them about gratitude and honor. Find joy in learning more about your Creator. Find more questions about God by asking great questions. May your life be about seeking to live in a way that brings more heaven to Earth.

How to Call Bullshit
and Other Charming Tactics

Bullshit. You can smell it. After a while, you can even see it coming. But learning to call it out is the magic trick to master.

When I was about eight, I heard my God-fearing, Bible-preaching, hospital-visiting grandfather cuss for the first time. He called bullshit—for the cows. Listen, my grandfather was all man: a rare mix of blue-collar strong and smart with a gift for making and maintaining friendships. He also was an independent Baptist preacher from the hollers of southern West Virginia—the kind of place where three hundred people and banana pudding is a big-time gathering that requires "special music" of the bluegrass type. So when I heard him call bullshit for the first time, I was shocked and excited all at the same time.

See, in the winter on the farm we used to serve the cows cattle feed that was mixed with dried chicken manure—I shit you not. And they ate it up! Every day. . . . One day, we are stocking the barn with bags and bags of this fine dish when my Papaw pauses and says, "Daryl, do you think the cows ever look at each other and say, 'I'm tired of eating this—this shit is bullshit.'" Swear to god, that phrase has stuck with me for nearly forty years: "I'm tired of eating this—this shit is bullshit." Part of the shock to an eight-year-old was your Papaw cussing (I did not think grandfathers did that), and part of it was that it was just really funny to imagine that the cows would finally figure out we were feeding them a bunch of shit. I've never forgotten it.

In your life, there are relationships where bullshit has to be called because it's toxic. There are relationships where bullshit has to be called because you love them and want them to grow. Then there is the bullshit that you know about yourself, that you often hide from others. Don't wallow in this; call it out in yourself. This is probably the hardest one, but it will be the best place to start.

Here is the lesson: Sometimes you have been fed so much bullshit that you forget you are eating it. You forget what the truth tastes like. Sometimes you need someone else to help you lift your head from the trough to really see it.

Exploding Cows and Collecting Bones

Your uncle Aaron had cows. Big cows. Purebred Simmental. Most of the adult female cows were over 1,400 pounds. Bulls were 2,000-plus pounds, no lie. Huge!

One of his prize-winning cows got into some crab apples, and it messed her up so bad that her stomach got all twisted up, and she passed away one night in the barn. But that's where the story begins. . . .

We had to move the carcass, and a small farm with one old Massey Ferguson tractor makes a plot worth watching. So, in the middle of the night, we began to attempt to drag this hunk-o-beef out of the barn to dispose of the body. Problem: It's stuck in the barn. Dead weight. So after wrapping heavy-duty crane straps around the cow's neck (hand-me-downs from Dad's job at the power company, of course) and multiple attempts, we were beginning to get what resembled a giraffe, to the point where I said out loud, "If the head comes off, I'm out of here!"

Aaron, at thirteen, looked like a tractor-pull champion on that old rig, riding a wheelie out of the barnyard and successfully dislodging the poor girl as we pulled her down the field to bury the body.

Challenge two: The tractor has no bucket. So how are we gonna dig a hole large enough? That's when Dad came up with the idea to reenact my favorite scene from *Conan the Barbarian*: the cremation. Burn the body— that was the idea at 10 p.m. that evening. So we started gathering anything flammable in the field. Keep in mind, we lived alone on about five hundred acres in West Virginia. There was no HOA. We piled up a large stack of old wooden pallets, boards, and a few old truck tires and covered it all in diesel fuel.

Dad lit the match. We sat back on the tailgate of our old Ford and watched a lot of hard work go up in flames.

At first, the smell of hair and flesh with the burning diesel was so strong you could barely breathe, but after an initial gag we settled in to watch the darkness with the bovine bonfire. Then it happened. . . .

It was about midnight when the first explosion came. It was startling. We were just staring, almost hypnotized by the flames, when it awoke us. POW. Then *blooop—bloop—bloooppp*. . . . All we could see was a stream coming out of and down the carcass—think volcano-like, with flickering fire flaming in the lava as it oozed down the pile of wood and bones.

"What was that?!" we shouted as we turned to Dad.

Almost like an old Western character, he turned to the glow of the fire and said, "Well, boys, that was her stomach. She's got three more to go. Y'all have a good night. I'm headed back up to the house."

WTF?!

The man didn't lie. As Aaron and I stood watch over the flames for the next couple of hours, we heard and saw the trifecta of tripe in the moonlight. We were done about 2 a.m.

The next day, we headed back out to the field to clean up the remains. The daylight showed smoldering pieces of wood, bits of tire belting, and the broken-down, charred bones that remained. It honestly looked like lost pieces of a dinosaur skeleton, blackened and strewn about. We re-piled what was still smoking and left the lump to finish burning down.

Over the week that followed, our old golden retriever Lodi proceeded to reassemble the cow's skeleton (to our mother's dismay) in the front yard of the farmhouse—one gigantic bone at a time.

The entire episode left me with three takeaways: Aaron lost something he had worked hard to raise because of bad apples, Dad needed our strength to get rid of the body, and cow stomachs, under the pressure of gas, explode! Oh, and if your kids are going to be antifragile, growing up on a farm/having animals is about the best way to get them used to life and death at a young age. ⌾

All Houses Are Huts

I've spent enough time in East Africa to tell you that huts, while basic, do the exact job of a house. They are made to keep the rain off your head, keep the sun off your back, and help keep your children from being eaten by a lion.

All houses are huts.

Your mom and I started traveling for mission work internationally in 2010—the year she was pregnant with Ella. Thailand, Uganda, Kenya, and India, on rotation. Your mom worked with an organization focused on human trafficking, and I was knee-deep in farming and microloans. We both saw the way the rest of the world looked at housing. Every time we returned home, our house felt odd. It was too big, with too much stuff.

So while all of our friends were having more kids and getting bigger houses, we decided to go smaller.

2,900 square feet, down to 2,200 square feet, down to 1,350 square feet. . . .

We bought a foreclosed HUD (Dept. of Housing and Urban Development) house for $42,000 and decided it was a perfect place to test our theory. It had been full of cats and mold. In fact, I found one of the cats, who was on the front porch in Google Earth Street View, half buried in the backyard!

It was a complete gut job inside and out, but we did it all on a budget with the help of some great friends and a lot of creativity. That bungalow changed us and the way we looked at living spaces. It also changed the way we looked at the cost of living. Our final monthly payment on that house, with two kids, was $350 (plus local taxes and insurance). While the space was small, it created a lot of margin in other areas—our finances, our time, and our minds. At the end of the experiment, we decided to sell the bungalow completely furnished. "Take our stuff! All of it!" Your mom hosted an open house, and in one weekend saw more than two hundred visitors. >

As a people, we let our lives expand
into the space we give it.

We waste space.

Same with time.

By the end of the weekend, we had seven offers. We had done previous real estate projects, but this one changed the way we looked at everything. It was all just stuff, and we sold it all with the house. The only thing that we couldn't replace was each other.

After that, we went on to redevelop hundreds of thousands of square feet of old buildings and houses in our community of Lynchburg, Virginia. And after your mom died, I decided to continue down this path of rebuilding and restoring forgotten homes and buildings. I believe there is a redemption story in all of the work we do.

Today, I still believe all houses are huts. I believe we as Americans often forget our purpose and attach ego and gluttony to what amounts to a pile of wood, brick, and electrical wiring. (I've done enough demo, trust me, I know). As a people, we let our lives expand into the space we give it. We waste space. Same with time. So when we have bigger houses, we just have more stuff. When we think we have more time, we waste it with things that don't matter. Choose well, not often.

Make your home and your time intentional. You will find that less waste will give you more margin, and that the real beauty in life comes from editing well. Your mom was a great editor.

Be Like a Tree, Be Antifragile

In the eighties, Biosphere 2 was built in Arizona. It was created to study life in perfect conditions and develop ways to harvest plants that would not harm the planet. The trees inside the biodome grew quickly, but once they reached a certain height, they fell over.

Trees need the stress of the wind for several reasons. It makes the cells of their trunks more flexible and also creates "stress wood" in the outer rings that can support the weight of the tree as it grows. Plus, the wind drives the roots of the tree to grow deeper. Those deeper roots keep the tree from falling in the storms that come their way.

You are the same. And while we as parents want to protect our children from stress and pain, both are needed to make you antifragile. Not just so you bounce back, but like the trees, so you form cell structure in your mind, body, and spirit that allows you to actually come back stronger and grow. If we don't allow the storms to blow on you, we run the risk of you becoming too rigid to bend with the weight life will bring.

My hope for you is to raise adults who, when put to the tests of life, look at them with a subtle grin as you lean into the weather with the mindset of your Nana, Rachel: that "This storm, too, will pass."

How to Face Death

There is no easy way around this one, guys. It's a guarantee. You will see and experience death. And growing up with animals is the on-ramp to that reality for kids.

Cats. Dogs. Chickens. Ducks. Quack, quack, quack. . . . It's not easy, but experiencing this helps kids understand both the beauty of life and the sharpness of death.

Don't hide death from your kids. When their pet dies, let them see it. Have them bury it with you. Reflect together. Don't lie to them about it going missing. Closing the loop in their brains, as painful as it may be, is key.

They will need this understanding for the bigger moments surrounding death, sooner than you think.

Don't hide death from your kids.
When their pet dies, let them see
it. Have them bury it with you.

Reflect together.

Spring Will Come

There will be seasons of winter. Real and cold. Your soul and bones will feel frozen. Numb. Nothing will move with ease. You will feel stuck.

Hold on. Spring will come.

Spring will come slowly at first. You will feel a small change in the temperature, but it will be fleeting. You will see new signs of life popping up, but they won't fill the landscape just yet. And then it will happen. You will open your eyes and find that new color is all around. Your world will feel reborn almost overnight, even though you'll still have recent memories of the cold. Nights will get warmer, days will have longer light.

Hold on. Spring will come.

Your Mom Died in Front of You— So Now What?

August 30, 2023, 6 a.m. The morning your mom died, I called you and your grandparents into the room within minutes of her passing. You stood there with me. Holding each other. Sobbing and screaming, "No, no, no."

Emmanuel woke and crawled into the medical bed beside her. "Mama is asleep," he chimed as he lay beside her one last time.

So now what?

You didn't get a sugar-coated version of death. You had to come face-to-face with it. Your worlds came to a halt in the moment, but the earth did not stop spinning. Ages thirteen, ten, and three—you each experienced the greatest loss across the spectrum of understanding.

I kept you out of school the following week. In the months to follow, your grades dipped. Emmanuel had attachment problems and feared being away from me for any period while constantly crying "Mama!" whenever he felt any physical pain. It was his cry for help. Ella went to counseling almost immediately. Easton slept in my bed with me until Christmas Eve, each night flipping through old pictures of your mom and scribbling notes or lyrics to help her make sense of the pain.

But you three did not stay in that space. You each navigated through it in your own way—with the help of close female friends. You grew more in six months than most adults do in a decade. By the summer, one year later, your physical and mental adaptations were evident to us all. Our home became an episode of *Fuller House* with guest stars almost nightly. We welcomed friends and family, coworkers, and drop-ins on the regular, with each episode more diverse and colorful than the one before. We were rebuilding something new, together. >

Proud? An understatement. I looked at each of you with a peer-like pride, and my parenting approach has followed that route ever since. How would you parent people you love and truly respect? Who had endured four years of daily trauma watching their mom go through surgery after surgery and living in fear of death? You give them more grace. You talk to them with care and interest. You pause to enjoy your time with them.

Still your dad? Always. Still willing to be the heavy? Sure. More likely to hold your hand and laugh than worry about having the "perfect" kid? You bet.

For the rest of your lives, you will carry that memory. The death of a parent. A memory most experience as adults, you formed early. For the rest of your lives, let it be a vivid reminder. Use it. Celebrate her. Sing of her. You will have an advantage. You will have already experienced the worst, and while the fragments of that pain may forever be lodged in your heart, the muscles you have built around it will make you stronger and more capable than your peers. You will manage life moving forward better than those around you. I have seen you do it already.

I will be here for as long as I am given; I will help guide and coach. But soon you won't even need that beyond the comfort of my voice. You're capable. You have already been tried by fire. You are still standing—even taller than before. Go, my children! Go!

Hope Is a Sewer Rat

At Johanna's memorial, her friend and spiritual sojourner, Jill, spoke about hope. It's a tough pill after watching your loved one die, but hope sometimes is all you have. Sure, hope is not a plan. And hope doesn't pay the bills. But in the darkest moments, hope keeps us alive. In the words of your mom's least-favorite biblical writer, Paul (I joke, kinda), without hope, "We are of all men most miserable."

So as Jill, inspired by the poem by Caitlin Seida, went on to remind us, in the deep ugly recesses of pain and sorrow lives a sewer rat of the soul, and that is hope. Getting by on the scraps and finding a way to survive when you need it the most.

> *"Hope is not some delicate, beautiful bird, Emily.*
> *It's a lowly little sewer rat. . . ."*
>
> —Caitlin Seida

Your mom wanted to be a famous journalist. I just wanted to make cool art. When we met, we both had good work ethics, but we didn't have the best financial sense. Your mom was a saver, but the queen of the fifty-dollar "hope in a bottle" type of purchase. I, on the other hand, have always been a "big toys" guy. When it comes to money, your mom was always afraid there would not be enough; I have always been the opposite. I feel like "They print it every day, you just need to find more of it." Maybe that's why we worked well together financially. But neither one of us knew anything about assets and liabilities or how to manage businesses or the right types of investments to make. It's all something we learned along the way from failing and then looking for better ways to not make the same mistakes.

I've had several major career-change moments because of my commitments to your mom. When she wanted to move or needed a change in her life/work, I would figure out a way to pivot. I always felt like saving our marriage was more important than what was on our W2s. I feel that way today about you guys, too—my presence is more important than my job title for you. It doesn't matter to you as kids what I do, it matters if I'm there.

As your dad, my job is to make a way for you. To provide the things you need and help you understand what you don't. To make sure your home is clean and safe and that you're certain there will be food when you're hungry. I can't promise big riches, but I can promise to teach you how to make the most out of nothing, and turn really shitty stuff into something worthy of market value.

You're gonna hear the same message on repeat from me for the rest of your lives: >

Work hard, tell the truth, and find value where no one else sees it. Oh, and learn the difference between long money and short money. You will work out the details as we go. Just remember that money = energy.

The truth is, in your life to come, you will find men and women much smarter than me to guide you in your fields of interest—mentors. Listen to them and learn from them. Teach me if I'm still around. Just know that I will be cheering for whatever honest career path you choose to take.

SIDE NOTE:

My first big financial win was at eleven years old. I sold a José Canseco insert baseball card for $200. I was rich! Listen, it didn't last long because I bought a motorcycle, but I learned a really important hustle lesson: I could turn items other people wanted into real cash if I knew what the market was looking for. As a teen, I went to work washing dishes at my aunt's office. I threw hay for farmers all summer and mowed grass—anything to earn my own money. Always working. The work ethic was there and so was the entrepreneurial understanding of market demand, but without reinvesting that money into assets, I was trading it for other things that had no long-term value. But did I mention that my junior high girlfriend thought my motorcycle was cool?

They Print It Every Day

A wise old guy once told me, "They print money every day, you just need to find more of it."

Look at money as pies. Some people think there is only one pie, and if you get more, they get less. I believe we can just go bake more pies.

Money is simply energy. We exchange it for services and products we want. You are in control of that exchange, remember; don't let it control you. Be kind, but don't be a sucker (or at least don't be a sucker twice). Be generous and always tip well after a meal or experience. You won't regret it later. Do it for yourself, but know people are watching how you handle your transactions.

When you start to feel stressed out about money, realize that it's really about fear and control. Take a hard look at what you're spending, plug the leaks, and then come up with a plan to bake some new pies.

Buying a Sheep in a Box

We used to go to a small country livestock market once every couple of months with Dad. The three of us would squeeze in across the bench seat of his old Ford and spend a Saturday afternoon in the smell and sounds of the Narrows County auction.

An old wooden ring of elevated benches encircled the cattle ring in the center. The dusty, dimly lit space was filled with whiffs of Beech-Nut chew and manure as the auctioneer was going at what seemed, to a kid, like a mile a minute. But the overall-clad old farmers had no trouble keeping up with what lot was up next. Our job was to sit quietly beside Dad while he waited for the right pair of steers to bid on. That's when it happened. . . .

The auction hands trotted some sheep through: "Sold!" And then they carried in a lamb in a box. We must have been twenty-five yards away from this little guy, but my brother Aaron was zoned in on him. His little seven-year-old hand shot up. My dad shot him a look to put his hand down, but he refused. The auctioneer took the opportunity to find a sucker and took my little brother's bid despite my dad telling him to put his hand down because no one else was bidding.

And then he just left his hand up. He was bidding against himself! Dad quickly yanked his arm down, but it was too late. We were now the proud owners of a lamb in a box. Not sure if you know this, but healthy lambs don't come in boxes.

So there we were on the ride home. No steers. One sick sheep in a box, riding home under Aaron's legs in the cab of the truck. He was smiling in the dark the whole way—I could see his toothy little grin.

The lamb wouldn't make it twenty-four hours. Aaron was upset. Dad was out about $25. That's a hard lesson as a kid because you want to save every hurt little creature you see, and at any market, you see lots of them. You think, "I can nurse it back to health." Truth is, most of the time, you can't.

Your uncle's heart has always been for animals. He went on to be a damn good rancher who has raised thousands of head of livestock. He has seen this story play out now hundreds of times. But we all learned a little lesson that night from his "little investment": the only lamb that should come home in a box is chops.

No One Cares How Early You Get Up

Your family will not care how early you get up, but they will care how late you get home.

Don't steal from your family.

Paying Tuition

When you fail, ask yourself, "What did I learn from the process?"

The hard fact is, at some point you will fail. A business, an investment, a project.

You will lose money. You will lose time. But don't lose faith in yourself.

Choose to look at the cost you paid as tuition. Think about what the best business schools would cost you for a year. Look at your loss of time and money and apply it to the bill. The key here is you have to learn something. Let real life be the best MBA program. It will be practical, not just theory—you will take away knowledge that is workable.

Lots of people pay tuition to go to school, but not everyone graduates. Pay the man and walk with your real-world MBA.

Cow Runs Over Dad

My dad really wanted to be a farmer. Truth is, he was a way better electrical engineer, but that didn't stop him from trying. The other thing you should know is that we didn't have any money growing up, so we did so much with so little for so long that we could do just about anything with nothing. That included hauling cattle in his 1968 Chevy C-10 2WD well-patinated, rotten-wooden-bed pickup. Imagine, if you will, cattle racks built out of decking one-by-sixes and two-by-fours mounted atop the rear of this rusty old pickup, sitting ready to receive a bovine at the end of a cattle shoot.

And so it was that one night at my grandfather's house (my grandfather also fashioned himself as a farmer—a better block mason than a farmer as well), alas, the two of them along with my uncle were trying to corral a cow up the shoot and into the back of the truck for market. The cow begins to go along with the plan, walking up the shoot and into the truck, and upon its hooves going through the rotten boards of the truck bed, it immediately turns around and starts coming back down the shoot.

When I say my dad tried, he really did. . . . He's not a big fella, but he put all 5'9" of himself in front of that charging cow to stop her and . . .

He lost. Bad.

My guy got *truuuuuucked* in the shoot. Think Ray-Lewis-with-a-running-start trucked. I thought he was dead. Like, another-world gonezo. . . .

He was not, and he picked himself up. Dusted off. Called it quits for the night. I'm pretty sure it broke his ribs, but he didn't complain much.

I can promise you this: We ate that cow not long after.

Deals Start in Third Grade

I once had an older business gentleman tell me he'd just closed a deal he started in third grade.

He was sixty-seven. That's a long time to work on one deal.

What he meant was, his character as a person—who he was in the community—had been known to be true for more than six decades. His consistency landed him a huge land deal sixty years later with his classmate from third grade. Often, we only think about right now, and it's so hard to imagine our true future selves, but if you're blessed with health, life is gonna be a marathon. Take the high-road, long-term approach to business and relationships.

Long Money vs. Short Money

Short money fixes "now" problems: bills, expenses, toys, and fun.
Long money ensures funds in the future.
Short money is often short-lived.
Long money is sticky and tends to make more of itself.

A great example is flipping a house vs. building a quadplex apartment that you hold onto. Yes, the $40–60K in your pocket feels good now. Yes, you can pay your bills with it, buy some tacos, and roll some of it into the next project, but the long-money approach of passive income acquired over the course of twenty years creates a constant cash flow that can also buy tacos. Meanwhile, someone else pays down your debt while increasing your equity position—for a future sale or to borrow against. Plus, you will get the ongoing tax benefits of depreciating the asset and claiming the expenses.

When you need cash now, play the short money, turn a profit, and get out.

But don't get stuck playing the short money game. Long money wins in the long run.

When you need cash now, play the short money, turn a profit, and get out...Don't get stuck playing the short money game. Long money wins in the long run.

Don't Cheat

Don't cheat at the register. Don't cheat in cards. Don't cheat on your spouse. And don't go into business with people who do. A cheater can't be a trusted partner.

The pain of the truth stings much less than the wounds of broken trust.

The More Important It Is,
the More Resistance You Will Feel

Your mom loved birthdays. She taught me how important they are to kids. In fact, a birthday party was the very last time we were all together as a family.

If we learned anything after your mom's death, it's that you are not guaranteed tomorrow. She was at Ella's birthday Sunday—days before she passed away—getting the last moments she could with you. That Sunday, she was determined to celebrate Ella's thirteenth birthday and your Pops' seventy-second. She was yellow and swollen. She had been retaining fluid for months after her liver stopped processing fluids correctly. She was gritting it out because she knew it might be her last. And it was. Don't miss the lesson. You are not promised tomorrow, only today. Choose the important stuff and get. It. Done.

If you don't want to do something, there is a good chance that's exactly the thing you should be doing. "I don't feel like it" and "I'llllll do that later" are signals that something needs to be the priority. In his book *The War of Art*, Steven Pressfield teaches that this experience is called "'the resistance," and it is evil by nature. It keeps you from moving forward with the thing you are most called to do.

When it comes to work, don't let anyone tell you that you're doing too much or you need to slow down. Those words often come from people who are lazy or scared. Pour yourself into the work, pour yourself into your family, pour yourself into your art, pour yourself into learning something new, and then know when it's time to turn it off for the day. Go home. Close the computer. Lay your tools down. Recharge with those you love and rest, knowing you did the best you could for that day, praying that God may grant you one more. Do not take tomorrow for granted.

Love What Loves You Back

This is tough. If you take a job, build a business, or sign a contract to do something you're fantastic at, at first things are great. You love the work. You pour yourself into it. You overcome some challenges and, if you're lucky, make progress and money along the way. And while the act of the work creates meaning in your life, the truth is, it does not love you back.

Midway through your mom's cancer, I quit my job. At the time, I had an executive marketing position at a company I loved. I loved the people and the work, but I knew you guys needed me—more of me. So walking away from it was an easy choice. There will be more work, but I had only one chance to raise you while caring for your mom, and I did not want your memories to be of your mom dying alone on the sofa while I was away on another business trip. It was the right call. I invested two and a half years at home with you and her in a season of continuous bouncing between doctors' appointments, surgeries, school stuff, and family field trips. We made memories and sucked all the life we could out of her last years with you.

I have no regrets. When she was laid to rest that day in our home, I felt a sense of pride amidst the pain. I knew we had finished well. I had honored her and my vows. I had done the work, paid the cost. In sickness and in health, till death.

Make it your goal to have a thousand people at your funeral. And maybe that will be a result of your work—your work with people—but not of your work itself. Your company's name will not be on your tombstone. So, while I want you to be loyal and very hardworking, I also want you to know when it's time to lay it down and focus on the people in your life. The ones who love you back.

Your company's name will
not be on your tombstone.

Snake Killers

I was about thirteen when we opened up a pit of "blowing vipers" on the farm. Yes, yes, they are also called hognoses or puff adders; you pick, but regardless, they are damn snakes.

We were cleaning up the field after the epic cow incineration, and upon flipping the remnants of a tire, we uncovered a snake hole. First one, a silvery blue devil, slithered on out hissing . . . *gag* . . . to immediately meet his fate at the end of a large crowbar. Then another and another. By the time we were done, my brother and I had massacred seven snakes—killed off a whole brood. It was a mess, but a good lesson. . . .

Snakes often don't lie alone. Where you find one, you will probably find another. Don't let your guard down after you get rid of the first.

The Leader Has to Know What They Want

The shelves of our house have been filled with books on leadership. I've read most—okay, at least the first forty pages of them—and the thing I think they all take for granted is the first and most basic question:

What do you want?

As the leader, you have to be able to answer this with clarity and confidence. What do you want? What do you want to build? What direction do you want to go in? If you're gonna lead, form the answer, write it down, and then make it simple enough to share and be repeatable.

Make the call. Make it fast. Ask a better question or two of people you trust, and then make the call. Often, we see leaders freeze when the rest of their team is waiting on them. Like cars backing up at a stoplight, everyone behind is waiting for you to pick a direction.

To lead means to have followers. If you don't know where you want to go, don't expect anyone else to.

...Life herself is a teacher. You can choose to humble yourself beforehand, or she will do it for you.

How to Be Taught (When I'm Not Here)

One day soon, I won't be here. All of the in-person teaching moments as a father will be gone. All that will remain will be your memories and these words.

Be teachable.

For the rest of your life, be teachable. Humble yourself enough to continue learning. You can learn something from everyone, even if it's what not to do. Find good mentors and friendships where you can trust the other person's counsel. Listen. Apply. Retry.

There will be moments in your work when you become the seasoned expert. It won't happen as soon as you think, but it will also sneak up on you. One day, you will look around and realize you have become the man or woman everyone is looking at to solve problems and have the answers. You will know that moment because it feels like being alone in a crowded room. Remember this: In that moment, pause, take a breath, ask better questions, and then pull the trigger. Your team/family will need you to be decisive.

But what if you make the wrong call? Be teachable.

You know this, but life herself is a teacher. You can choose to humble yourself beforehand, or she will do it for you.

THE END.
(FOR NOW)

To Whom

A quick note of thanks to:

To Blue Hat Publishing—specifically Brandon and Rachael—thank you. Brandon, thank you for reaching out after Jo's death to let me know you had walked the same path and I would be OK. Rachael, in the midst of your own cancer journey you helped me bring this book to life. I pray daily for your peace and wisdom.

To my Lynchburg community of friends - I am so grateful for you collectively. There are far too many to name individually, but you know who showed up - when Johanna needed your love and care - you showed up. You created space and gave resources so she could try and find healing in her soul and her body. As I considered moving after her death, the community we have here - (beautifully messy but connected and caring) made me choose to stay. And as long as I'm here, we have work to do!

Thank you to - Adrian and Alisha - you both have made every effort over the last two decades to keep us all connected. Alisha you have given AP and I time to work on our relationship and sharpen each other. We are both better because of your love.

To my oldest friend - Chris Carroll - I am a better man because of your consistency and the fact your family adopted another white kid on the weekends.

Thank you to - Brandon & Brittany - I am grateful for business partners and friends who at some point became more like family. We carry on the legacy left behind for us and the kids. May we always journey to discover the small gems - all the while laughing out loud together.

To the people who said yes - Jim & Rachel - thank you for giving me your blessing to marry Johanna, and then you followed it up by supporting us both - consistently - thank you for always showing up for us and the kids for more than 20 years. Thank you for teaching us all to continue learning and unlearning who God is and how we can bring more Kingdom to Earth.

Thank you to - Ralph and Charlotte (Papaw & Mamaw) - for showing me what committed and playful love looks like. I know that I am a direct reflection of you both. Your love of me as the oldest of many grandkids was not wasted - I've always known I was your favorite. I promise not to tell the others.

Grateful for my parents - Russell and Diahn - who created a safe home for us as messy young boys. Thank you for cheering for us from the bleachers consistently and teaching us to fix stuff that we broke.

To the lady who picked up my poop and gave me my first job - Carolyn - so grateful for your laughter and presence in my developmental years. You were the best aunt a boy could ever want!

Thank you to my brothers - Aaron and Joel - for making a childhood worth telling and retelling. You are both men of integrity and honor - I am so proud of you both.

And finally to the woman who truly showed up for my children and I when we needed it most - Erica - thank you for loving us and adopting the four of us. You have returned beauty and joy to our home. Our story is one of redemption for us all. I love you, we love you beyond...

In his professional life, Daryl Calfee has been an art director, a marketing executive, a community-minded property developer, and a damn good mechanic. Then there's his real job: raising two beautiful, creative teenage girls and a room-brightening, monster-truck-loving preschooler. Their family is daily invested in the small community of Lynchburg, VA.

To learn more and connect with Daryl, visit www.DarylCalfee.com.

www.ingramcontent.com/pod-product-compliance
Lightning Source LLC
Chambersburg PA
CBHW070124100426
42744CB00010B/1909